ESSENTIAL FINANCE

DIVORCE AND FINANCES

SARAH PENNELLS
AND
MARC ROBINSON

21·03·04

LONDON, NEW YORK, MUNICH,
MELBOURNE, DELHI

Project Editor Richard Gilbert
Senior Art Editor Sarah Cowley

DTP Designer Rajen Shah
Production Controller Sarah Sherlock

Managing Editor Adèle Hayward
Managing Art Editor Marianne Markham
Category Publisher Stephanie Jackson

Produced for Dorling Kindersley by
PORTAL PUBLISHING
43 Stanley Street, Brighton
East Sussex BN2 0GP

Creative Director Caroline Marklew
Editorial Director Lorraine Turner

First published in Great Britain in 2003
by Dorling Kindersley Limited,
80 Strand, London WC2R 0RL

A Penguin company

2 4 6 8 10 9 7 5 3 1

Copyright © 2003
Dorling Kindersley Limited, London

Text copyright © 2003
Sarah Pennells
and Marc Robinson

A CIP catalogue record for this book is available
from the British Library

ISBN 0 7513 3726 9

Reproduced by Colourscan, Singapore
Printed in Hong Kong by Wing King Tong

See our complete catalogue at
www.dk.com

CONTENTS

INTRODUCTION

Britain has one of the highest divorce rates in Europe. Dealing with divorce is one of the most stressful experiences that anyone can go through and one that many people believe they will avoid. Sadly for some, the reality is different. Finding yourself negotiating – or even worse arguing – with someone you thought you would spend the rest of your life with is hard enough. Being faced with unfamiliar legal terms and processes and having to make long-term decisions about your financial future makes it even harder. Divorce and Finances is designed to help you through this potentially overwhelming task, particularly if you have not had an active role in the day-to-day management of the family finances. It will tell you what to expect and will help you make the right decisions for your financial health both during and beyond divorce.

GETTING AN OVERVIEW

Money issues are also life issues. When you decide to divorce, every aspect of your financial life becomes involved in the separation between you and your soon-to-be ex-spouse.

SPLITTING ONE HOUSEHOLD INTO TWO

The overall issue is how to take the resources you have used to run one home and divide them in order to run two. There is no escaping this fact: dividing everything ultimately leaves less for two single people than what was available to a married couple.

DIVIDING EVERYTHING

Splitting your resources can have profound implications for you and your ex-spouse's standard of living. The outcome will affect many parts of your life including where you live, where you work, what you do, and what you can afford to do. When you file for divorce, the financial considerations focus around two main areas: the family home and maintenance.

RESOLVING OWNERSHIP OF YOUR HOME

Your home is likely to be the most valuable asset, and you will almost certainly have formed a great emotional attachment to it. There are no hard and fast rules about who gets the home – it will either be down to you or the courts to decide. It could be that one spouse remains in the home, or that you each have to buy a new – and smaller – property. Also, many divorcing couples will not own their property outright, but will have a mortgage. That will need unravelling before new financial arrangements can be made.

The court system requires both parties to make a "full and frank" disclosure of their finances.

CALCULATING MAINTENANCE

It is less usual for maintenance to be paid where there are no children. Usually, in this situation, couples opt for a "clean break" settlement. However, with older couples where one spouse (usually the wife) has not worked and it is too late for her to start a career, maintenance may be paid. The Child Support Agency (CSA) will probably get involved in calculating maintenance payments where there are children. You will both have to make sacrifices and you may find that agreeing maintenance is far from easy.

KNOWING WHEN TO USE A SOLICITOR

Just as a marriage is a legally binding contract between two people, a divorce is, first and foremost, a business deal. No matter how emotional you may feel now, it is wise to keep that in mind.

> **2** A specialist divorce solicitor will be best qualified to represent your interests.

HIRING A SOLICITOR

If you think you have less experience than your spouse in financial, legal, or business issues, it would be wise to hire a solicitor to help you protect all of your interests, especially if you have children. You may start out thinking you can do the whole thing yourself but, unless you are on very good terms with your spouse, you will probably need professional help at some point. Solicitors can cost from around £150 per hour upwards, so it may pay to shop around.

If you think you cannot afford to hire a solicitor to represent you, you may at least want to pay for an hour's consultation to gain an overview of your rights and obligations. Find a solicitor who is mindful of your goals. You may find it useful to ask for recommendations from other people who have been through divorce. Try not to use your solicitor as your therapist, however; keep it as professional as you can.

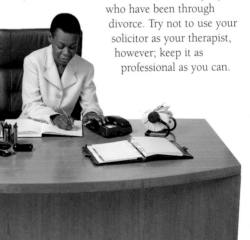

DOING IT YOURSELF

In rare instances – for example if you are divorcing without animosity, you do not have children, you own a simple set of assets, and you both earn comparable incomes – you may be able to get by without professional assistance. But whether you go about dividing your assets amicably or not, make sure that you get a final order drawn up, which says that your claims against each other are dismissed at that point.

Document everything. It would be wise to document everything you do in case a problem arises later. You will need records of each of your assets and perhaps a document stating that you both disclosed your finances in a "full and frank" way. Even if the documents are determined not to be legally binding, they may help you clarify issues later.

Stay informed. It still makes sense to read this book and other resources on divorce so that you understand all the issues involved.

Know when to seek help. Often divorce is not straightforward and involves a range of potentially complex issues. It may involve more than simply dividing assets, such as maintenance for your children or for you (or your spouse). In addition, business interests and other assets, such as pensions, can be important. In such cases, you should seek legal advice.

AVOIDING THE INFLEXIBILITY TRAP

The more money you spend fighting (in other words, paying solicitors and other professionals), the less you will have left. The less you have to split, the less flexible you can be. The less flexible you are, the longer you can expect it to take to settle disputes. The longer it takes to settle disputes, the more you will spend on the fight. The result can be a vicious circle.

HIRING A MEDIATOR

Mediators do not represent either spouse. They listen to both sides and try to help you reach an agreement that both of you can accept. You will still need to hire a solicitor to turn it into a legal document. Many mediators are solicitors who specialize in divorce or who have some legal background. It can be quicker and cheaper than going down the legal route because costs are shared. Family mediators will help with issues of child custody and access during a divorce.

USING MEDIATION

Mediation is becoming increasingly popular as a way of dealing with divorce, but many people are still not aware that it is an option. It should not be confused with reconciliation – it is about reaching agreement on the divorce.

CONSIDERING MEDIATION

You do not have to use a solicitor and the court process to negotiate your divorce. Even though many lawyers stress that the court system itself can be quite amicable, you could consider mediation instead. It can save time and money, which inevitably means less stress.

ARRANGING FINANCE THROUGH MEDIATION

Mediation can deal with a whole range of issues surrounding divorce, including child care, property, and financial matters. It is confidential and impartial and does not exclude you from going to court at a later date. Anything said during a mediation session cannot be used in court, although documents can be used.

3 People getting help with the legal costs of their divorce have to attend one mediation session.

EXPLORING HOW MEDIATION WORKS

Sessions with mediators normally last for around 90 minutes and most couples have between four and six sessions. There is often more than one mediator present at the session and many have some legal training. They will not tell you what is right or wrong, but will try to ensure that both of you have a fair say. Ideally, you and your spouse should have the session together, but if there are reasons why that cannot happen, you can still use mediation – mediators simply ensure that both partners are in separate rooms. Do not think it is merely taking the soft option: it can be very difficult to be in the same room when you are both feeling emotional. However, if you can deal with the emotional side, there are benefits. Mediation has the advantage of letting couples have more control over the process and can reduce hostility. There is no guarantee of success, however, and if your spouse will not co-operate, you may have to turn to the courts after all.

THINGS TO KNOW

- You normally pay for your mediation at the end of each session. Many divorcing couples split the cost between them.

- If you cannot agree, you will have to contact a solicitor, but at least after the mediation sessions you may have a clearer idea of where compromises can be made.

- Many mediators with legal training are members of the Solicitors' Family Law Association. You can get details of someone who may be able to help you by telephoning 01689 850227 or logging on to www.sfla.co.uk.

- Both spouses set the agenda for sessions, so if one was dominant during the marriage, it may not work.

TALKING IT THROUGH ▲

Coming face to face with your spouse during a mediation session is something that some people may find just too difficult. However, although the mediators will not take sides, they are skilled in ensuring that both parties get to have their say during the discussions.

GETTING IT ▼
WRITTEN DOWN

If you reach an agreement, it is important to have it recorded in writing. You can then take it to your solicitor as the basis for a legal document.

GOING TO COURT

If you cannot work out amicably who gets what and you have to go to court, you may find yourself rather bewildered by the process. There are no standard rules about who is entitled to what, so you should not necessarily expect a better deal just because you contest it in court.

TAKING THE FIRST STEPS

Getting divorced, even in the most straightforward circumstances, will take some time. You will certainly feel that your emotional life is in flux, and your finances could come out much worse as well. Sorting out money may be your last priority, but do not put it off.

SPLITTING THE ASSETS

Dividing property and possessions that you have accumulated during your married life can be one of the most stressful parts of a divorce. With emotions running high, it is impossible to be objective about where the division should be made. However, do not forget that, unless you can sort things out between you, you are likely to run up large legal bills. In some cases, these bills could add up to more than the disputed items themselves, so try to keep things in perspective. Some people manage to reach a financial settlement before they get to court, but if you cannot, the court will take certain factors into account in determining how all the assets are to be divided.

These factors include:
- The length of the marriage.
- Each spouse's age and health.
- Each spouse's earning capacity.
- Standard of living when married.
- The contribution each spouse made to the family.
- The value of a benefit, such as a pension, which either spouse would lose the chance of acquiring as a result of the divorce.
- Each spouse's financial needs, obligations, and responsibilities.

▼ AVOIDING COURT
It is always better to try to reach a settlement before you go to court, in order to avoid costly and protracted court proceedings.

4 Financial proceedings in court do not have to be hostile. They can be arranged amicably.

KEEPING WHAT IS YOURS

Whatever you brought to the marriage individually – in financial and property terms – is not ring-fenced. How it is treated depends largely on how long you have been married. The longer the marriage, the less important your original financial input. The court is also less likely to order the sale of a family heirloom, but the same may not apply to other assets (including money and investments). However, the debts owed by one person before marriage will probably be considered that person's sole responsibility.

PAYING FOR CHILDREN

The needs of any dependent children always come first. These days, most maintenance agreements will be sorted out by the CSA. When it was first set up, it worked to a very complicated formula about how much should be paid to the parent looking after the children (usually the mother). Radical changes are now being made to ensure that a percentage of the absent parent's net income is allocated to each child. In limited circumstances, you can ask the court to decide maintenance.

PREVENTING SALE OF ASSETS

If you think your spouse is about to try to get rid of assets, you can apply to the court to prevent him or her from doing so. This procedure normally requires a solicitor so, if you do not already have one, you should instruct one. Likewise, if your home is owned solely by your spouse, you should register a charge on it. It is possible to do this through the Land Registry without your spouse being informed. Registration of your rights does not mean that the property will automatically not be sold, but it does indicate to other parties that you have a financial interest in it. In practice it would be difficult for them to sell or remortgage it, because the party who has the interest would have to be informed.

DOES FAULT MATTER?

In very few cases of "extreme" conduct, the court *may* consider a spouse's fault in causing the divorce when deciding how to distribute the property and settle maintenance. However, it is very rare, so be wary of making any assumptions about it forming part of your settlement. It is best to consult your solicitor first.

IDENTIFYING KEY DATES

There are several landmark dates in any divorce proceedings. Knowing what they are and what they mean will leave you better equipped to deal with the whole process. At this stage, the fewer surprises the better.

DATE OF MARRIAGE

Your wedding date is considered as the date your marriage began and you normally need to have been married for a period of time before you can divorce. Then you must show that the marriage has irretrievably broken down on one or more of the following grounds:

- Adultery.
- Unreasonable behaviour.
- Desertion for two years.
- Separation for two years, with spouse's agreement to divorce.
- Separation for at least five years, when the consent of your spouse is not needed.

DATE OF PETITION

This is the date that you file the divorce petition in court. The "petition" is a form that you fill in and which is then served on the other party, who has to acknowledge receipt. You cannot get divorced without a petition. Once one party (the "petitioner") has filled it in, the form has to be filed in court. At the same time, if there are children involved, a "statement of arrangements" form will have to be filled in. This includes details of where the children will live and whether maintenance has been arranged. The court or solicitor will then serve the petition on the spouse, who also has to say whether or not he or she consents to the divorce. If adultery is alleged and the third party is named, that person will also receive a copy of the petition.

5 Do not forget to let the relevant organizations know if you change your name after the divorce.

DATE OF DECREE NISI

The court will tell you when the *decree nisi* will be pronounced. It does not mean that you are divorced, but it is a major step. Both you and your spouse will be sent a copy.

DATE OF DECREE ABSOLUTE

You can apply for a decree absolute six weeks and one day after the *decree nisi* has been pronounced. Until you receive the decree absolute, you are still officially married. In extreme circumstances, you can apply for the decree to be made absolute before six weeks and one day have elapsed. When it becomes absolute, you and your now ex-spouse will each be sent a copy and you are divorced.

DIVORCING BEFORE THE SETTLEMENT

Can you be divorced before you finalize your financial settlement? The answer is definitely "yes". The typical case is one where one spouse wants to remarry before all the issues such as child maintenance, access, and distribution of property have been resolved. Whether it is in the other spouse's interests to do so is open to question. Many solicitors caution against applying for a decree absolute until the finances have been sorted out. This is particularly important for the spouse who is currently more financially dependent on the other party. For example, if the other party were to die after the divorce but before the settlement, the dependent ex-spouse could be left with very little.

6 Try to agree the date of separation with your spouse for tax purposes.

NEGOTIATING YOUR FINANCES

Any good negotiator will tell you that good preparation is vital to achieving your goals. You can help yourself by knowing where you are now and where you want to be.

CREATING A BUDGET

Budgeting and saving are the two basic principles of personal financial management. Anyone who takes the time to create a budget during divorce will be in a much better position to negotiate.

▼ REVIEWING EXPENSES
When drawing up your budget, remember to include an estimate of how much you will need to replace large household items such as furniture or computer equipment.

ALLOWING FOR ONE-OFF EXPENSES

If you are the one moving out, include in your budget the cash you will need for a deposit on rent or a down payment to buy a new home. You may also need cash to restock household supplies or to buy furniture, appliances, and other large items. If you shared a car, you may want to have an idea of how much a down payment would be for a second car. Even if you are not moving out, gauging these costs will help you judge how reasonable your spouse is being when requesting money for these items. You may also have to restock items that become your spouse's property.

CALCULATING REGULAR EXPENSES

Calculate daily living expenses, such as running the household, child care, dry cleaning, petrol for the car, pet food, and regular maintenance of your home. It will be easier to do if you keep a diary of your expenditure, preferably for a month. It is easy to overlook "minor" expenses, but they can all add up. For example, it is easy to forget expenses such as daily newspapers or subscriptions to magazines, so make sure you include these items.

BUDGETING FOR INTERMITTENT BILLS

Nearly everyone has expenses that arise infrequently, possibly only once each year. Many people forget these items when budgeting. For example:
Car. There may be repairs, new tyres, MOT, and road tax.
Healthcare. This may include dental treatment, spectacles, or contact lenses. If you have pets, do not forget to include vet's bills.
Activities. Consider expenses, such as activity holidays and sports clubs, for you as well as for your children.

---

7 Once you have a record of your spending, it should be easier to make savings.

SAVING MONEY: TIPS FROM THE EXPERTS

Many experts recommend strategies to build savings. Remember that cutting costs is an instant way to save money. If possible, add those savings to the money you put away and invest.

- Be disciplined. Live within your means.
- Save at least 10% of your salary. Consider yourself as one of your own creditors – pay yourself first.
- Use your credit cards less. If you have a credit card with a high interest rate, try transferring the balance to a new credit card with a low interest rate (there are many competitive offers on the internet, for example).
- Monitor how often you eat out. For many people, this expense turns out to be considerably more than they realize.
- Consider term insurance instead of whole-of-life insurance. It is cheaper and useful if you need it to cover a specific period (for example, mortgage term or children's schooling).
- Shop around for all your insurance, whether it is for your car, your home, or contents. You should also consider raising the excess levels on contents or buildings policies.
- Put your money into investments that will help you reach your goals, such as a deposit account to build up emergency cash, income-producing bonds, or share-based investments for capital growth over the longer term.

USING A WORKSHEET

W*orking out how much you will need to live on should not be a guess. Take the time to list the expenses you are likely to face, and work out how much they will cost on a monthly basis. It is important not to leave anything out. This worksheet should give you a head start.*

HOUSING EXPENSES

Rent/mortgage _____
Endowment/ISA _____
Council tax _____
Service charge _____
Gardening _____
Housekeeping _____
Household repairs _____
Painting/decorating _____
Furniture, accessories, linens _____
Cleaning supplies _____

UTILITIES

Water charges _____
Electricity _____
Telephone _____
Gas _____
Appliances and upkeep _____

TRAVEL EXPENSES

Car payments _____
Car repairs _____
Road tax _____
Fuel/oil _____
Public transport _____

PERSONAL EXPENSES

Food _____
Clothing _____
Laundry _____
Dry cleaning _____
Toiletries _____
Books _____
Magazines _____
Newspapers _____
Cigarettes _____
Gifts _____
Hair _____
Lunches at work _____
Courses _____
Career training _____
Hobbies _____

INSURANCE

Car _____
Buildings _____
Contents _____
Life _____
Income protection/
critical illness _____
Mortgage protection _____

MEDICAL EXPENSES

Private medical insurance _____
Dental _____
Optical _____
Prescriptions _____
Other medicines _____

ENTERTAINMENT

Holidays and travel _____
Cinema _____
Videos _____
Theatre _____

DINING OUT

Restaurants _____
Parties/entertaining _____

MISCELLANEOUS

Credit card debt _____
Hire purchase _____
Other loans _____
_____
Charitable donations _____
Subscriptions _____

TAXES

Income _____
VAT _____
Capital gains _____

CHILDREN

School fees _____
School trips/holidays _____
Babysitter/child care _____
Pocket money _____
Travel to school _____
Maintenance _____
Tuition _____
School uniform _____
Books and other
equipment (such as
pens, pencils, calculator) _____
Sporting goods _____

OTHER

(fill in with your own entries)

_____ _____
_____ _____
_____ _____
_____ _____

TOTAL _____

COLLECTING RECORDS

D*ivorce negotiations often come down to having a clear, full picture of your financial status as a married couple, and to supporting the arguments you decide to make.*

STORING INFORMATION

Copy. Make copies of all financial records, including wills, trusts, and the last few years of tax returns.

Record. Write down the names, addresses, account numbers, and balances of all bank, building society, insurance, and credit card accounts, and all pension details. Store them in a safe place away from your copies.

Verify. Check what is in your safe deposit box (if you have one) and write down the contents. You may want to take pictures, as well.

DOCUMENTING INCOME

Review your income from past years (some experts recommend going back at least five years). This can be vital to negotiating support amounts and for discovering any money that may have been hidden from you.

Pay. Look at recent pay slips, if available, and make copies. Try to get at least five slips.

Statements. Collect at least several years' worth of bank statements so you can document when and where all income was spent, or how much of it was spent. Credit card statements are also helpful.

Other income. If you or your spouse received income from investments, renting property, bonuses, or from any other sources, you should document them.

KEEPING A RECORD OF SPENDING

C*redit card receipts can help determine the type of lifestyle each person had during the marriage. Records showing a long pattern of spending indicate a consistent lifestyle. Records showing only recent spending may indicate change.*

8 Keeping an organized filing system will save your accountant or solicitor time, which will end up saving you money.

REVIEWING ASSETS

Cars. Check that your car is in good working order. For all cars, look at the registration documents to see if they are owned jointly or just by you or your spouse. Review the car insurance to see whose name is on the policy.

Insurance. Review all insurance policies relating to your home, the furnishings in the home, and personal belongings of value. If any items were individually valued, detail them in your records along with the financial account information. Include photocopies of all valuations (such as for your home and valuables).

Property. Review documents relating to any property you may own. List who owns it, when it was purchased (before or after the marriage), who contributed what, the purchase price, any outstanding mortgages and other secured loans, and any income derived from it (including when the income is received).

Make copies of all:
● Deeds.
● Mortgages or other secured loans.
● Rental agreements.
● Tax records.
● Valuations.

IDENTIFYING OTHER USEFUL DOCUMENTS

Life insurance. The policy will explain how you or your spouse will be protected if one of you dies.

Prenuptial agreement. These vary depending on where you live. For example, in England and Wales, they carry little weight. They do not exist in Northern Ireland. They are taken into consideration in Scotland, but are not guaranteed to be binding.

Passports. These may show times when your spouse left the country and could possibly have deposited assets elsewhere.

Wills. If you are going for a divorce, you should make a new will, or vary the one you have got. Keep your existing one for reference.

Business documents. If you and/or your spouse own a company or are part of a partnership, the documents that formed those entities can help determine present and future values of marital assets. Also look for profit and loss statements (P&Ls), balance sheets, or similar documents.

9 If you take documents relating to your spouse's financial situation, you have to let your spouse know.

REVIEWING CREDIT

A credit reference file is a factual account of your borrowing and paying habits. It is important to order a copy to verify that what is being reported about you is current and correct. The file could also alert you to potential problems that could affect your own credit rating.

ASSESSING YOUR CREDIT RATING

One of the most common problems after divorce is credit history, because any activity on a joint account is the responsibility of both spouses. Many spouses, for example, do "last minute" shopping through their joint accounts before announcing a separation. Any failure to repay becomes a joint failure to pay and is likely to end up on your individual credit reference files. Check the statements of every joint account carefully, then telephone to check spending after the statements were issued. Finally, either close the accounts or change them to individual status.

GETTING HELP

The Information Commissioner's Office has produced a booklet called *No Credit?*, which is available by telephoning 01625 545745, or logging on to the website at www.informationcommissioner.gov.uk.

OBTAINING YOUR CREDIT FILE

You are legally entitled to see your credit reference file as often as you wish, and to know how certain items got there. Many people order a copy before they apply for a loan, in order to resolve any problems before a lender sees the report. Each credit reference agency stores different information, so get a copy of your file from each agency. The agencies will charge a small fee for your file, so check the current amount before you apply.

10 People who do not have accounts in their name may find it difficult to get credit on their own.

IDENTIFYING ERRORS

Mistakes do happen, or it may be a case of information you do not recognize. Files can carry data about relatives or ex-spouses with whom you have no financial connection. Ask the agency to remove their details. If you do not recognize the name of a credit company, check your agreement. Some companies use third parties to operate their credit agreements. Since negative information can remain on your file for up to six years, it is worth spending the time making sure your file is correct.

THINGS TO KNOW

- **Supplying the right information.** In order to get a copy of your credit file, you will need to give the agency your date of birth, your current address, and any other addresses over the last six years.

- **Disputing mistakes.** Errors are inevitable. If you think information is wrong, you should contact the credit reference agency in writing. The agency should immediately mark the information as "disputed" on your file, so that a lender cannot take it into account. Agencies should deal with queries within 28 days of receipt.

- **Acting on a refusal.** If you are refused credit, the lender does not have to tell you why you were turned down, and you do not have a right to credit in the first place. However, if data held on your credit file led to a refusal, the lender has to give you the name and address of the agency used.

- **Staying in touch.** Keep in contact with creditors if you are facing problems making your repayments. With good communication, many creditors will try to work with you – for example by not reporting a late payment to the credit reference agencies so that the least possible damage will be caused.

MAKING CONTACT

Here are the credit reference agencies and their contact details:

Equifax
Credit File Advice Centre
PO Box 3001
Glasgow G81 2DT
Tel: 0870 514 3700
Website: www.equifax.co.uk

Experian Limited
Consumer Help Service
PO Box 8000
Nottingham NG1 5GX
Tel: 0870 241 6212
Website: www.uk.experian.com

Callcredit PLC
Consumer Services Team
PO Box 491
Leeds LS1 5XX
Tel: 0870 0601414
Website: www.callcredit.plc.uk

CHECKING YOUR CREDIT FILE

*W*hen you are going through a divorce, it is particularly important to check your credit file so that you can identify any errors or negative items that may have arisen.

READING YOUR FILE

When you receive a copy of your credit file, check it thoroughly and note any errors. If you think that there is no basis for an entry, you can write to the credit reference agency and ask for it to be removed. If an entry is incorrect, you can ask for it to be removed or amended, stating why you think the entry is incorrect. The agency should respond within 28 days of receiving your letter. If the entry has been amended, the agency will send a copy to you.

DEALING WITH NEGATIVE DATA

A large amount of positive information can sometimes outweigh negative data, especially if the debt was small, was incurred some time ago, and has since been paid off. Otherwise, you can deal with a negative item as follows:

- Pay off the outstanding balance and then ask the creditor to update your credit file accordingly.
- Wait for the negative item to be removed from your file.
- Write an explanation of the debt and ask the credit reference agency to add it to your file. The negative item will not be removed from your file, but future creditors must take your explanation into consideration.

Files from different agencies may vary in appearance and often carry information from different lenders.

SAMPLE CREDIT FILE

Electoral Roll Information
This acts as confirmation of your address and how long you have lived there. It is a legal requirement to register.

ELECTORAL ROLL INFORMATION
At: 12 Old Drive, Anytown, WX1 2YZ

Lawrence, Tom	97 – 03
Lawrence, Linda	97 – 03
Singh, Rajinder	90 – 97

Search Information
When you apply for credit, a company will carry out a search on your name. This shows which companies searched your file.

SEARCH INFORMATION
At: 12 Old Drive, Anytown, WX1 2YZ

Record Date:	15/02/03
Search Type:	Credit Enquiry
Client Name:	ACME Finance Co.
1st Applicant Details:	
Name:	Mr. Tom Lawrence
2nd Applicant Details	
Name:	Mrs. Linda Lawrence

Court Information
This section includes a list of any County Court Judgments (CCJs) registered against you, how much they were for, and when the debt was paid off.

COURT INFORMATION
At: 12 Old Drive, Anytown, WX1 2YZ

Court Date:	29/04/98
Case Number:	12345678
Court Name:	Anytown
Judgment Value:	£432.00
Defendant:	Mr. Tom Lawrence
Satisfied:	24/08/01

Insight Information
This records your payment history on outstanding loans and other credit. The information is supplied by the lenders.

INSIGHT INFORMATION
At: 12 Old Drive, Anytown, WX1 2YZ

ACME Credit Card	Mrs. Linda Lawrence	
Terms:	Monthly	
Balances:	Limit:	£3,000
	Outstanding:	£360.48
	Written off:	£00.00
Effective Dates:	Start:	05/12/02
	End:	
Monthly Status:	00000000000000	
Insight Last Updated:	06/05/03	

Monthly Status
This reveals whether you have made your monthly payments on time. The row of zeros shows that payments were made on time.

Insight Last Update
This shows how recently the information was updated.

Outstanding
This shows how much is still owed on the loan or credit agreement, according to the lender's last update.

SEPARATING JOINT ACCOUNTS

As soon as possible after separating, you may want to manage all of your finances through your own accounts. The easier it is to show separate money, the fewer conflicts there may be over who has rights to that money.

PROTECTING YOUR BANK FUNDS

When couples have a joint bank account and begin divorce proceedings, they should close the account or transfer it to a single name account, otherwise both parties will be liable for any debts incurred. If you inform your bank that you are undergoing a divorce or are in dispute, the bank will generally contact both parties and may arrange a joint interview so that each can specify which payments (such as direct debits and standing orders) should still be made. Alternatively, upon notification of divorce, the bank will cancel the "mandate" that allows a single signature to authorize transactions. From that date, all transactions will have to be agreed by both parties. Closure of the account would also need agreement from both parties. In a more amicable situation, you might decide to take half of the money each and deposit it into new, separate accounts. Whatever your situation, however, you should take steps to protect your money, otherwise your spouse may use all of it and leave you to negotiate its return. Inevitably, it is easier to negotiate from a position of strength than one of weakness.

DEALING WITH CREDIT CARDS

There is no such thing as a joint credit card, but it is possible that you and your spouse may each have a credit card from the same agreement. The procedure varies between different card issuers but, broadly, if you are the principal cardholder (the person who signed the original agreement), you should contact the card issuer by both telephone and post and explain the situation. The card issuer may ask you to destroy the secondary cardholder's card. The company will then either close your account and set up a new one in your name alone or, if you are satisfied that the secondary card has been destroyed, allow you to keep the existing account open. If so, do not forget to cancel direct debits or standing orders that your spouse may have set up. One word of caution: if you cancel a card, remember that you may leave your ex-spouse without adequate spending capability. That may cause irritation or anger, and negotiations could become more difficult as a result.

12	Responsibility for joint debts incurred during your marriage will continue even after you are divorced.

CHECKING YOUR OTHER CARDS

It is important that you check your charge cards and store cards. It may be that an account was opened mainly for the secondary cardholder's benefit. However, regardless of who uses the account the most, it is the person who signed the credit agreement who is responsible for the debt, so tell the card issuer about the situation as soon as possible.

SECURING A SAFE DEPOSIT BOX

A safe deposit box can easily be emptied by the other keyholder without your knowledge. Whoever gets there first has the upper hand. You probably have little chance of recovering the items that were in the safe deposit box, which can have emotional as well as financial consequences, since many people keep sentimental items in safe deposit boxes. To safeguard your interests, you must inform the bank of your circumstances. As with joint bank accounts, once you have informed the bank of your separation or divorce, the bank will normally revoke the original mandate and will refuse to open a safe deposit box without both partners being present.

FINDING HELP

You do not have to face your financial future on your own. Many professionals and organizations can be of assistance.

VISITING YOUR BANK

If you do not have an accountant, or if he or she is working for your spouse, consider visiting your bank manager, especially if you have a good relationship with your bank in your own right. Bear in mind, however, that your bank manager can sell only a limited range of products, so you may be better off with an independent financial adviser.

USING FINANCIAL ADVISERS

If you have a financial adviser, he or she should have a thorough understanding of your financial situation. However, you may feel uncomfortable dealing with the adviser if that person also advises your spouse. Either way, it is worth talking to someone who can give you advice on your overall position. Bear in mind that, if you want a review of your position and do not want to buy any financial products, you may have to pay a fee for the adviser's time.

CONSULTING A DEBT COUNSELLOR

If you find you are having problems managing on a reduced income, try consulting a debt counsellor. You do not have to pay for it. Organizations such as the Citizen's Advice Bureau offer free, confidential advice.

HIRING AN ACCOUNTANT

Your accountant can help you make use of all the available tax allowances, protect your privacy, maximize the use of any assets, find ways to help you increase your income, assist with managing finances, and help you find other qualified professionals to support your financial goals.

USING FORENSIC ACCOUNTANTS

Forensic accountants are specialists who can be useful during divorce. They are typically hired to determine current and future values of assets where reasonable people could disagree. For example:

- Valuing loss of pension rights.
- Calculating the worth of businesses, companies, and shareholdings.
- Determining a true level of a spouse's income from accounts.
- Analyzing the ability of the spouse to raise a lump sum.

MAKING SURE MAINTENANCE IS PAID

Many problems are caused by maintenance payments either not starting when they are meant to or stopping for no reason. If the Child Support Agency has made an assessment and given a date for payments to start, and the money does not appear, it has fairly wide-ranging powers to try to recover the money from the former spouse. It is able to:

- Go to court to make the former spouse pay maintenance. This can even include sending in bailiffs to take possessions up to the value of the money owed, or securing court orders against property or other assets such as savings accounts. In the case of property it means that, when it is sold, the proceeds will be released up to the value of the money owed. Likewise, with bank or building society accounts, an order can require the release of funds up to the value of the money owed.
- Withhold benefits. If the former spouse is claiming Income Support or Job Seeker's Allowance, part of the benefit can be deducted directly in order to pay maintenance.
- Ask the employer of the former spouse to deduct the money directly from wages before they are paid.

LOGGING ON TO HELPFUL WEBSITES

Child Support Agency. This website (www.csa.gov.uk) includes information about how the CSA works, how it makes its assessments, and gives answers to frequently asked questions.

National Council for One Parent Families. At this site you can find useful fact files on a range of subjects together with contact details of other agencies that can help parents during divorce. You can get access to these files by logging on to www.oneparentfamilies.org.uk.

Independent Financial Advisers. There are several websites where you can find an IFA. The Society of Financial Advisers (SOFA) lists IFAs who have a degree-level qualification (called the Advanced Financial Planning Certificate). Log on to www.sofa.org and click on the "find an adviser" section. Alternatively, you can find an IFA through www.unbiased.co.uk.

DIVIDING ASSETS AND DEBTS

One of the most important, and potentially volatile, aspects of a divorce involves identifying all assets and debts, valuing them, and determining how they will be divided.

UNDERSTANDING HOW COURTS VIEW PROPERTY

The courts may order a property to be sold and the proceeds divided in two, but that is not the only option open to them.

LIVING IN RENTED ACCOMMODATION

If you live in rented property, you may be able to transfer your tenancy to your spouse. Tenancies that qualify are assured tenancies under the Housing Act 1988, secure tenancies under the Housing Act 1985, statutory tenancies under the Rent Act 1976, and protected and statutory tenancies under the Rent Act 1977. If the tenancy is in your spouse's name and he or she has left you, you must ask the court to transfer the tenancy before the divorce.

OWNING YOUR HOME

If you own your home, then the way the courts treat it will often largely depend on whether or not you have children. Many people wrongly believe that the home will be divided according to who paid what towards its purchase and upkeep. However, that is often not the case. There are circumstances where it may be relevant, for example if there are no children and it is a short marriage, in which case the courts may consider each partner's individual contribution to the purchase and upkeep of the home. The longer the marriage, however, the less important the financial investment made by one spouse becomes. If the property needs to be sold in order for both spouses to be in a position to afford new homes, then that is what the court is likely to order.

13 If you cannot afford the mortgage repayments, it is much better to sell up and move on than to struggle.

LOOKING AFTER CHILDREN'S NEEDS

The accommodation needs of the children are of utmost importance. The courts would be unlikely to order that the family home should be sold unless there is enough money to buy another property that would be large enough for their needs. What they may arrange is for the property to be sold at a later date, for example, when the youngest child leaves school (called a *measure order*). The home may be transferred to the name of the spouse who will be living there, or it might be sold and the proceeds divided in the percentage agreed. If it is not sold at the time, a charge will be put on it so that money can be repaid when the property is eventually sold.

ENSURING STABILITY

Many parents try to make sure that the children have as much stability as possible about where they live, at least until important schooling is finished. However, it is not always possible.

ORGANIZING YOUR HOME

A home is typically one of the largest family assets, or at least one of the largest issues, in divorce. The emotion of having to leave your home or possibly having to sell it to make ends meet can make difficult financial issues even more tricky to handle.

STAYING IN THE HOME

If you can reach an amicable arrangement, it may be less distressing – particularly if there are children involved – for one partner to stay in the family home. This is not always practical, however. If there is not enough money for your spouse to buy another property, you may have to sell. If you are staying, you may have to keep up the mortgage repayments, either from your own money or from maintenance payments. Repair bills, insurance, and council tax must also be taken into account.

14 If you want to stay in the area, remember that many markets are localized, meaning that prices can vary sharply.

GETTING HELP FROM A GUARANTOR

If you experience difficulty getting the lender to agree to one of you taking over responsibility for the whole mortgage, you could ask a family member or friend to act as a guarantor. The person you choose should take legal advice first, however, because he or she could be pursued for payments if you fail to make them.

MOVING OUT

Just because you leave the family home does not mean an automatic end to your responsibilities. If you have a joint mortgage, you will not be able to get your name removed from the agreement unless the lender is satisfied that the person remaining can afford to keep up the repayments. A common solution, particularly if there are no children involved or if they are older, is to sell up and each buy something smaller. It is unlikely to be an ideal solution for either of you, particularly if you have lived in the family home for a long time or spent a lot of effort and money improving it.

CONSIDERING OTHER ISSUES

● With joint mortgages, the lender should keep both parties informed. If you suspect your ex-spouse is not making repayments, you can request a statement.

● You may agree to sell your interest in your home to your ex-spouse instead of selling the home outright. It would be your ex-spouse's responsibility to demonstrate to the lender that he or she could make the mortgage repayments or, if necessary, remortgage with a different lender.

● If you are trying to get a mortgage and you are relying mainly on maintenance payments for income, you may struggle. Many lenders will not count maintenance payments as income, even if they are backed by a court order. There are exceptions, however, and some lenders will treat individual cases more sympathetically. Contact a mortgage broker, who will know which lenders to approach.

● If you find yourselves in a stalemate about who will leave and who will remain in the home, you may lose the right to resolve the issue to the satisfaction of either party. The court may simply order you to sell the home and divide the proceeds.

SELLING YOUR HOME

*I*f you own your home, it may be more valuable for the cash it can generate from a sale than as a residence. With two households to support, you may decide that the best course of action is to sell your home and divide the proceeds.

CASHING IN YOUR INVESTMENT

Selling your home does not just involve dealing with the bricks and mortar and getting a joint mortgage turned into a sole one. If you have an interest-only mortgage and there is an endowment policy running alongside to pay off the loan, it can be more complicated. You will have to get a valuation of your policy and decide whether one of you can continue paying into it, or if it makes more sense to cash it in and split the proceeds. If you cash it in, you will lose any terminal bonus that might have been paid at the end of the term, and you will also lose the life insurance cover. If your health has deteriorated since you took out the policy, you could find it difficult or expensive to get another policy.

Cashing in does mean you may not get back what you paid into it, especially if you do so in the early years. You could get 10–30% more by selling it on the secondhand market, if it has been running for more than seven years, but not all policies qualify. It is worth taking advice on this, because making the wrong move could leave you thousands of pounds worse off.

SETTLING A REPAYMENT LOAN

The situation is much more straightforward with a repayment mortgage. You simply ask the lender for an up-to-date statement of how much is owed and pay it off. If you are on a fixed, discount, or capped rate, there may be penalties for redeeming the loan early, so check with your lender. There may also be life insurance to consider.

◀ MOVING HOME
Your share of the proceeds may not go far after paying your portion of professional fees and removal costs.

ARRANGING TO SELL THE HOME

You will need to agree about:

- Which estate agent you will use.
- What the preferred selling price will be.
- What the lowest selling price will be.

You will also need to agree that the person remaining in the home will co-operate with estate agents and potential buyers and will keep the home presentable at all times during the selling period.

HANDLING OTHER INVESTMENTS

Pension-linked mortgages are not very common, and were mainly sold to people paying the higher rate of tax who were likely to continue their self-employed status (and therefore could not join a company pension). The idea was to build up enough capital to pay off the loan at retirement and provide a pension. The pension does not have to be stopped just because it is no longer being used to pay off a home loan. Other investment vehicles, such as ISAs (Individual Savings Accounts), and their predecessors, PEPs (Personal Equity Plans), are much simpler to deal with, mainly because they cannot be held jointly. Unlike an endowment, the policy does not run for a specific term, so there are no penalties for cashing it in early. However, depending on the level of the stock market at that time, you may lose out if you do cash it in. It is in your best interests, therefore, to seek qualified independent advice first.

15 Write to your endowment provider first if you are considering changes to the policy.

DEALING WITH A BUSINESS

You may not want to be a business partner with your ex-spouse after a divorce. After all, most people say that partnerships are like a marriage.

ENDING THE BUSINESS RELATIONSHIP

Dividing a business can be very complicated. Expert assistance is required to determine how much the business is worth, what liabilities it may face, and more. Here are some general ideas about dividing a business on divorce.

If one spouse owns the business. A court will not usually force a spouse to sell a business if it is the spouse's primary source of income. This becomes an even stronger argument if that income is also the primary means for paying maintenance.

If both spouses are owners. You will both have to decide whether to continue your working relationship despite ending the marital relationship. Typically, one spouse will buy out the other's portion of ownership. This could be structured in one of several ways:

- Make an all-cash payment. This keeps the deal simple.
- Pay cash in instalments. Until the buyout is complete, the spouse who is selling could hold the business as security in case the buying spouse defaults on the payments.
- Trade the business ownership for another asset (such as a home) – or series of assets – of equal value to the business.

THINGS TO CONSIDER

Here are some questions to ask:

- How is ownership of the business held and what type of ownership is it (for example, share ownership, sole proprietorship, partnership)?
- Is there an opportunity for each spouse to form separate businesses by splitting up the existing business?
- Were you involved in the business primarily for tax reasons, or did you make a real contribution to its worth?
- What is the value of the business interest for purposes of a divorce?
- What income tax liabilities come with ownership of the business interest?
- What other property or assets are available that could be used to offset the value of the business interest?

16 Consider whether you want children to retain a share in the business. If so, seek professional advice.

GATHERING DOCUMENTS

Here is a list of some documents you may need when valuing and dividing a jointly owned business:

- Income tax returns for the past three years.
- Financial statements for the past three years.
- Interim financial statements since the last year-end statements.
- An inventory of assets and each asset's location and current market value.
- Valuations of any assets.
- Any letters of intent or purchase offers that you have received during the past three years.
- Any buy-sell agreements or partnership agreements.
- Forecast or budget for the current year's trading.
- List of other shareholders and their number of shares.
- A breakdown of directors' remuneration, detailing basic pay, bonuses, and benefits in kind.
- Lists of any abnormal events, income, or expenditure in the last three years.
- Details of any private expenditure put through the accounts.
- Lists of bank facilities, actual balances outstanding, and security given for loans.
- List of top ten customers and the percentage each customer provides of total sales.
- Any special purchasing agreements or service agreements with a vendor.
- Non-competition agreements.
- Loans payable to shareholders, partners, or owners.
- Loans receivable from shareholders, partners, or owners.
- Any trust deeds or other documents containing information about how you acquired your ownership interest in the business.
- Any trust deeds or other documents showing current ownership structure or future ownership structure.
- List of any loans or debts of the business that you or your ex-spouse have personally guaranteed.
- List of any perquisites or benefits that the company provides for you, your ex-spouse, and for your children or other family members and the cost to the company for providing the perquisite or benefit.
- Any business valuations that were done during the past three years.

VALUING A BUSINESS

The value of a jointly owned business can play a significant role in the overall division of property. Finding common ground on the value of the business and how to divide it is often one of the most contested – and expensive – aspects of divorce.

DECIDING ITS TRUE VALUE

Valuing a publicly quoted company is comparatively straightforward. However, if it is a private business, it is much more difficult. There is a variety of standards an accountant or solicitor might use to determine the value of the business. If it is comparatively small, you and your ex-spouse's solicitors may be able to agree on a figure that satisfies everyone. If the business is very valuable or complex, a forensic accountant may be necessary. Either way, there are several methods that can be employed.

Earnings basis. With this method, the valuer looks at the profit stream that the business could earn in the future. He or she will then apply an appropriate multiple to those profits, often benchmarked to similar quoted and private companies. Economic and other factors are also taken into account. For example, if the firm is owned by both parties, could it survive if one of them left? Does it have too high a level of borrowing?

Assets basis. This is suitable for businesses where the trading is in large assets. To get a valuation, the accountant would look at what would happen if the business was liquidated. Since this often involves property valuation, a surveyor is normally used as well.

Cash flow basis. This is uncommon for divorce valuations. The valuer considers the cash received, rather than profitability. However, many businesses do not prepare cash flow forecasts and it may be too "precise" for divorce courts.

Dividend yield basis. This can be useful for valuing a minority shareholding. These shares may not be worth much on the open market, but a larger shareholder may want to buy them to increase his or her shareholding.

RECOGNIZING GOODWILL

With many service-based businesses, such as doctors', accountants', and solicitors' practices, goodwill will be recognized as a component in determining their value. Ask your solicitor if it is relevant.

---

17 If your ex-spouse will not co-operate in providing the books, ask for a court order.

PREPARING FORECASTS

Smaller businesses may not have prepared financial forecasts for their own use. However, these are useful if you want to have an idea of the future worth of the business. Getting hold of information that shows how the company has done historically is easier, but may not be relevant.

Check the purpose. If the financial forecast was prepared in anticipation of getting a bank loan, it may differ from statements prepared for tax purposes.

ASSESSING INTANGIBLES

Most businesses are affected by intangible factors that could alter their value. Some examples are goodwill, patents, and trademarks. Calculations to value these in isolation can be complex, and you can expect them to differ. Often these items are absorbed within the earnings basis valuation. You may also find that the results differ depending on whether your accountant or your ex-spouse's accountant is doing the calculations, so be prepared to negotiate.

TAPPING INTO RETIREMENT ASSETS

Assets from retirement plans can be a significant portion of the marital property to be divided. Changes in the law in the last few years mean there are several options for divorcing couples.

UNDERSTANDING PENSION PLANS

There are two main categories of pension plans.

Company pension schemes. Not all company schemes are the same. With some, called "final salary" or "defined benefit" plans, the amount of money employees get at retirement depends on their salary and the generosity of the scheme. The pension amount is not affected by stock market returns. With "defined contribution" or "money purchase" schemes, the amount employees will have on retirement depends on the investment performance of their pension fund.

Personal and stakeholder pensions. You do not have to be an employee to have a personal or stakeholder pension. You can be self-employed or, in the case

of a stakeholder, you can have no earnings at all and still save for your retirement (there are limits to this, however, so check with your tax office or an independent financial adviser). As with money purchase plans, the amount you get at retirement depends on how well the fund has performed.

▼ **UNLOCKING YOUR WEALTH**
Do not underestimate the power of a pension. Many divorcing couples prioritize what will happen to the family home, but unlocking the value of a pension can be more financially rewarding.

18 A pensions solution for someone else may not be the best one for you, so take expert advice.

GETTING A PENSION VALUATION

If you have a personal or stakeholder pension, write to the provider for a fund valuation. For a company pension, you should contact the trustees.

DIVIDING THE PENSION

Although the value of the pension has been included in divorce settlements since the 1970s, it has often been overlooked. Since December 2000, the pension can be divided at the time of the divorce, through pensions sharing. The three pensions options are as follows.

Pensions offsetting. With this method, the value of the pension fund is offset against other assets, such as the home or other investments. It has the advantage of being straightforward, but is not always the most transparent way of dealing with such an important asset.

Pensions earmarking. Part of the pension fund (both the lump sum taken at retirement and the income) is set aside for one spouse to take when the other spouse retires. The disadvantage of earmarking is that, if the pension scheme member (or policyholder) dies before he or she reaches retirement age, so does the ex-spouse's entitlement to any regular income. The ex-spouse would only have a claim on part of the lump sum. The same would apply if the ex-spouse were to remarry.

Pensions sharing. The pension fund is divided at the time of divorce. If the spouse with the pension is a member of a company pension scheme, the other spouse may be admitted as a member in his or her own right, but this varies from employer to employer. More commonly spouses receive money to use for their own retirement plans.

INCREASING THE STATE PENSION

It is possible for a spouse to increase his or her state pension by using the former partner's National Insurance contribution record. The amount he or she will get depends on the length of the marriage and the divorce date.

19 The older you are, the more important the pension is likely to be.

DEALING WITH INSURANCE

You need to think about your insurance requirements. Where there have been joint policies, you will probably have to take out individual ones.

ARRANGING LIFE INSURANCE

You may be trying to cut down your expenses post-divorce, but do not neglect vital insurance. Mortgage lenders may insist on life insurance to cover a loan. For anyone with children (unless they are grown up), adequate life insurance is a must. If you have a joint policy, it is probably better for one spouse to take it over, than to take out two new policies. Circumstances can vary, however, so consult your independent financial adviser. Do not just think about replacing lost income. With child care a major expense, the spouse who is not caring for the children should also consider a policy that will pay for child care in the event of the main carer's death. It is possible to take out a life insurance policy that will pay out a lump sum, or one that will provide a monthly income.

PROTECTING YOUR MORTGAGE PAYMENTS

Your mortgage protection insurance is designed to pay the mortgage in the event of redundancy or sickness. However, it is often only taken out by the main wage earner. If that party leaves and the remaining spouse takes over the mortgage, that person may be advised to take out a policy in his or her own right. Some lenders insist on it as a condition of the loan. However, it can be up to 50% more expensive than one taken out at the time the mortgage was arranged.

INSURING YOUR CAR

Check to see if you have been a named driver rather than the policyholder during your marriage. If you have, some insurers will still offer you the same level of no claims discount as your ex-spouse enjoyed. You must meet certain criteria, however, such as having been on your spouse's insurance for a qualifying period.

PRESERVING MAINTENANCE PAYMENTS

If your ex-spouse is required to support you or your children, you may want to guarantee that maintenance continues with a life insurance policy to cover payments should your ex-spouse die. As long as you have an "insurable interest" in someone's life, you are within your rights to take out a policy to cover the loss you would suffer.

TREATING WHOLE-OF-LIFE POLICIES AS ASSETS

If you or your spouse have a whole-of-life insurance policy, it may have a cash surrender value, meaning that you can receive cash if you end the policy before dying. The policy may also let you borrow against the cash value, making it a valuable asset in time of need.

CONTINUING YOUR MEDICAL INSURANCE

Your ex-spouse may have a generous package of employee benefits. Losing these, or your entitlement to be included in them, can have a significant impact on your finances. These often include private medical insurance (PMI), which the whole family can use. There are different rules about whether you will be able to continue on that policy after divorce. It often depends on both the insurance provider and the employer. Most conventional policies are purely for the employee and a spouse or partner who lives at the same address. If you cannot benefit from your ex-spouse's policy, you could try to negotiate a lump sum in order to continue with a similar one. Your solicitor or an independent financial adviser can advise you on its value. However, comparisons can be difficult and it should be borne in mind that company-sponsored private medical insurance traditionally has higher benefits for psychiatric problems than individual policies have.

20 If money is tight, prioritize your insurance needs. Then start building up an insurance fund.

FINDING HIDDEN ASSETS

If someone has been planning a divorce for a while, and if that person is so inclined, he or she might devise numerous strategies for hiding money from a spouse and children. With the right legal help, however, it is possible to find these assets, but it can be expensive and time-consuming.

PURSUING ASSETS

Many people spend a lot of time and money in solicitors' fees, arguing over particular assets, only to discover that the assets were not worth fighting over in the first place. Before you spend a lot of money, get an expert forensic accountant on board to determine the merits of pursuing them at the beginning of the process. A suspicion that your spouse is hiding assets does not necessarily mean it will be worth spending money to find them.

21 Question whether pursuing an asset might cost more than the value of the asset itself.

▼ **TAKING ADVICE**
Listen to what the professionals have to say about whether there is a realistic opportunity to find or recover an asset. They will probably have dealt with many similar cases to yours in the past.

WORKING OUT THE COST

If you get a forensic accountant involved, you could spend anything from £1,000 to £20,000 or more, depending on complexity and the value of the assets in question. As with all professionals, the better prepared you are before you see them, the lower the eventual bill will be. Take as much documentation with you as you can. Make a note of anything that backs up your claim.

UNRAVELLING INVESTMENTS

While it is comparatively easy to value a holding in a quoted company, if a spouse has invested in a private company or in joint ventures, that can be much more difficult to quantify accurately. There is a similar difficulty with any offshore investments. The actual cost involved could have been small, but the investment may be quite valuable or profitable. Pensions are another area where money may be hidden. For example, the accounts may show that £20,000 has been invested, but the pension fund you are aware of may reveal only a £10,000 contribution.

22 Bills being settled from unknown sources may indicate an undisclosed bank account.

SPOTTING THE TRICKS

If you have a business, here are some tricks you, your solicitor, or a forensic accountant will look for to see whether your spouse has disclosed all business assets:

Secret bank accounts. Opening accounts without letting the other spouse know.

Provisions in accounts. Marking down expenses without any intention of spending the money.

Overpaying the boss. Paying the boss a generous salary, which is hard to demonstrate as being "too high".

Underpaying the boss. The owner or managers may suddenly cut their salary dramatically in the run-up to the divorce.

Overpaying "workers". Paying a girlfriend or boyfriend a large salary through the business.

Undisclosed income. Setting up a management company that then charges the main business for its time – siphoning money out of the "known" business.

Friends as business partners. Setting up a second company as above, but using friends to front it.

Business hitting hard times. Pretending that the fortunes of the company have deteriorated in order to reduce the valuation of the business and the subsequent payout to the ex-spouse.

GETTING YOUR SHARE OF STATE BENEFITS

G etting divorced may mean that you are eligible for certain benefits that you could not claim while married. It may also have an impact on which party claims tax credits designed to help with the cost of children.

UNDERSTANDING THE NEW TAX CREDITS

There are various benefits or tax credits available, which you or your ex-spouse could already be receiving. The most relevant of these are Child Benefit, Working Tax Credit, and Child Tax Credit. Until recently, Working Tax Credit and Child Tax Credit were known as Working Families' Tax Credit and Children's Tax Credit. The idea behind the reorganization of the Working Families' Tax Credit and the Children's Tax Credit is that it enables all the child-related credits to be made in one payment, namely the Child Tax Credit. Many organizations have welcomed the change, but there are concerns that some people may not make a claim because they are unaware that they will qualify. If you are in any doubt about your entitlement, check with your local Inland Revenue office first.

CLAIMING BENEFITS AND TAX CREDITS

Child Benefit. If you are responsible for a child under 16 years of age (or between 16 and 19 if in full-time education), you may be able to claim child benefit. This is a weekly benefit and is normally paid to the primary carer of the children. Divorcing couples can decide between them who gets it and, if they cannot agree, it will be handled on a case-by-case basis by the Benefits Agency.

Child Tax Credit. This is means-tested and based on the income of the highest earner within the couple. In any one tax year, either you or your spouse could earn up to a certain salary and still receive the credit. Ask your tax office for the current salary limit. If you divorce, you can still claim if you have a child (or children) under 16 living with you for part of the year. The credit cannot be split if one of you pays tax at the higher rate.

Working Tax Credit. Workers on a low income (including lone parents) with children can claim this. It is paid as a credit in your payslip and, like other tax credits, is administered by the Inland Revenue, not the Benefits Agency. You cannot claim if you have savings over a certain amount. The amount of the claim depends on the number of children, income, and child care costs.

▲ CLAIMING FOR CHILDREN
The changes to the tax credit system mean that far more families are now eligible to claim state help. The majority of parents will now qualify for the Child Tax Credit – even higher-rate taxpayers.

PAYING THE CARER

The Child Tax Credit is paid to the main carer rather than the highest wage earner. It is based on a couple's combined income. To check your eligibility for this tax credit and how much you can claim, ask your tax office for advice.

23 If you think you may be eligible for the Child Tax Credit, contact the Inland Revenue or check with your accountant.

SPLITTING DEBTS

For many couples, getting divorced involves dividing debts as well as assets. There are basic guidelines, but not all of them may apply.

> **24** Finances are most often the cause of arguments between couples and can contribute to divorce.

DECIDING WHO IS RESPONSIBLE

Generally a spouse will not be held responsible for debts incurred solely by the other spouse. So if your ex-spouse had a car loan or a credit card, it is up to him or her to pay it off. Some bills, such as council tax, are the responsibility of the other party if they go unpaid. That means if your spouse leaves and he or she normally pays the

council tax, you must contact the council as soon as possible to stop the bill running up in your name. If you have joint gas, electricity, or telephone bills, you are both responsible for the outstanding amount.

Taking over responsibility. If you want to take over a gas or electricity account in your name only, you should contact the company and arrange for a meter reading. It should be straightforward if you are the one staying on in the family home, but if you move to a new address and have not had credit in your own name, you could face problems.

◄ **FACING UP TO DEBTS**
Do not be tempted to ignore letters from your bank or credit card company at a time like this. You will probably be feeling very fragile and emotional, and dealing with your debts may be the last thing you want to face. The problem will not go away, however, and companies are used to dealing with couples who are going through a divorce.

THINGS TO DO

As soon as you know you are separating:

- Make a list of all current debts, especially credit cards. Analyze the interest rate of each loan and card. Create a written plan to start reducing or eliminating these debts.

- Close all credit card accounts where there is a secondary cardholder and open new separate accounts. Inform card issuers of accounts you are closing that you are separating. Request that the issuer state that you closed the account so it does not appear to be closed because of bad debt.

- Inform any other lenders that you have separated and that you do not want any changes in the loan to occur without your permission. Ask for current balances and the type of account.

- List when each loan began and the reason why you and/or your ex-spouse received it. Include who has been making the repayments, the monthly amount paid, and the amount currently owed to the lender.

PURSUING DEBTORS

Creditors are not bound by the terms of a divorce agreement, so even if you divide the joint debts between you, they can pursue either party for the full amount. However, lenders are more likely to pursue the person who remains in the family home, because that person is easier to track down. With utility companies, if an ex-spouse with unpaid bills leaves, the other party could be pursued for the outstanding amount.

WATCHING YOUR CREDIT

Negative credit marks accumulated by one ex-spouse may affect the other person's ability to get credit, without the other person realizing it.

ACCEPTING JOINT LIABILITY

If both spouses co-signed for a debt, or if a debt was incurred through a joint account, both spouses will probably have *joint and several liability* for the debt. The term means that each spouse is individually responsible for the entire debt if that debt is not repaid.

25 Prioritize debts. Do not simply pay creditors who make the most demands.

DETERMINING MAINTENANCE

If children are involved, divorce usually involves determining
how much one spouse will pay to the other to help with child care.
Less commonly, a spouse with no children may receive payments.

SUPPORTING CHILDREN

The Child Support
Agency (CSA) was
set up in the 1990s to take
maintenance decisions
away from the courts. In
the early years it seemed
to do little but attract
criticism – either from so-
called "absent parents"
(usually fathers), who said
the CSA was pursuing them
for too much – or from
those parents left looking
after the children, who said
the agency was inefficient
and was taking far too
long to deal with them.

CALCULATING LEVELS OF MAINTENANCE

Since the CSA was supposed to recover some of the
benefits paid to lone parents, the formula it used for
assessing maintenance was linked to benefit levels,
and figures were adjusted every year. The complex
formula made errors more likely, and figures could
not be checked easily. The
CSA also struggled with
the volume of work and
lengthy delays built up.

APPLYING FOR MAINTENANCE

Not everyone has to have their maintenance application dealt with by the CSA, but when the parent with care is claiming Income Support or Job Seeker's Allowance, he or she must use the CSA. Other people can use the courts instead. Where divorcing couples can agree maintenance, it can be made into a court order "by consent", which can be varied by the court later. Many solicitors advise their clients to have a court order for maintenance drawn up, which they can ask the court to vary if necessary.

LOOKING AFTER THE CHILDREN

Parents' first and primary obligation is to support their children according to their ability to pay. The interest of children is usually the court's top priority. The purpose of child support is to ensure that the children will share in the standard of living of both parents regardless of where the children live or which parent cares for them.

27 A non-resident parent who earns under a certain amount will pay a flat maintenance rate. Check for current rates.

26 There can be no CSA assessment where a court order was drawn up before 5 April 1993, unless it has been discharged by a court.

CHANGING THE FORMULA

New rules governing the CSA have been produced and are gradually being introduced, along with a new formula for calculating maintenance. The new assessment formula is much simpler than the old one. It is hoped that because of this, parents will be able to check whether they are receiving or paying the correct amount and assessments should be processed much more quickly. Maintenance liability is based on an amount of the non-resident parent's net income: 15% for one child, 20% for two children, and 25% for three or more children. Lone parents on Income Support may be able to keep some maintenance, so ask for details.

LOOKING AFTER CHILDREN

The old ideas of child custody were replaced, in the Children Act of 1989, by parental responsibility. The courts can still get involved, but the aim of the reforms was to encourage divorcing parents to sort out the arrangements themselves. Where the children live has an obvious impact on the financial arrangements.

INVOLVING COURTS

Although you will be encouraged to sort out in an amicable way where your children spend their time, the courts can get involved. They can do so at the request of either parent, a third party (such as grandparents), and without anyone making an application for a court order.

SPLITTING TIME AND EXPENSES

There is no rigid formula about how much time your children spend with you and how much maintenance you are therefore likely to receive or have to pay. If you are the non-resident parent, you are still expected to contribute to the expense of raising your children. The CSA starting point is that non-resident parents should plan their lives on the basis of the income they have left after meeting their responsibilities to their children. If you have other children living with you, whom you are supporting financially (for example, if you are in a new relationship and have children with your new partner, or help provide for his or her children from a previous relationship), you may not be expected to contribute as much financially. You may agree to pay for certain expenses directly, which gives you more control over where the money goes.

INCREASING EXPENSES AS CHILDREN GROW

Bear in mind that raising children costs more as they get older and their universe expands. Their toys become more complicated (for example computers and even cars). They need more clothes. They may go to private school, where costs typically increase annually. As a single parent, you may need child care. There are after-school activities, entertainment, birthday parties, holidays, extra tuition, and other unplanned expenses.

◀ SUPPORTING THE MAIN CARER
In general, if you are the one receiving child maintenance, the more time a child lives in your home, the more money you will be entitled to receive.

SHARING EQUALLY

If your children live in both homes, the relative incomes of both parties may require one spouse to pay maintenance to the other. You may be able to come to an arrangement where you are each responsible for the expenses your children incur while they are with you and you may want to share certain expenses. Make sure that you do not try to use the arrangement to get at your ex-spouse. Do not be tempted to "outdo" your ex-spouse financially. You will probably be feeling a lot of guilt or anger about what has happened, but do not try to buy your children's understanding.

---

28 Courts can dismiss a spouse's claims, but children can claim in their own right.

AGREEING LEVELS OF MAINTENANCE

You can agree any amount you wish for child maintenance, if you are not using the CSA. If, however, either party decides that he or she no longer likes the agreement, the court has the power to vary it.

HOW LONG DOES MAINTENANCE LAST?

Although you can agree otherwise, child maintenance generally ends when the child reaches 17 years of age or leaves full-time education. However, certain situations could trigger an earlier end to child maintenance. For example, your child could marry, enter the armed forces, or take a full-time job. If the child switches homes, and lives full time with the other parent, child maintenance could end – or the payments could be reversed.

SUPPORTING A SPOUSE

Whether a spouse gets maintenance in his or her own right usually depends on age and personal circumstances. It is entirely separate from child maintenance. A court may decide that you should receive money for life, although payments usually stop after a number of years. Alternatively, maintenance can be paid as a lump sum instead of in instalments.

PAYING SPOUSAL MAINTENANCE

Like maintenance for the children, the ongoing maintenance an ex-spouse receives will normally be paid weekly or monthly. It is meant to give the person a steady stream of income to help pay for both the usual and unexpected costs of daily living. The courts have a reasonable amount of discretion in deciding how much should be paid and for how long, but there are some basic principles.

No gender issues. The spouse receiving maintenance can be a man or a woman. Maintenance is related to income capabilities, not gender.

Tax issues. Maintenance payments used to attract tax relief, but that has been abolished, except for couples where one ex-spouse was born before 5 April 1935. Payments received do not count as income for tax purposes.

Remarriage issue. When the person receiving maintenance remarries, payments will stop. Typically, payments will also stop after the recipient cohabits for more than six months.

29 Negotiating disputes will save you from court orders that could end up pleasing neither you nor your ex-spouse.

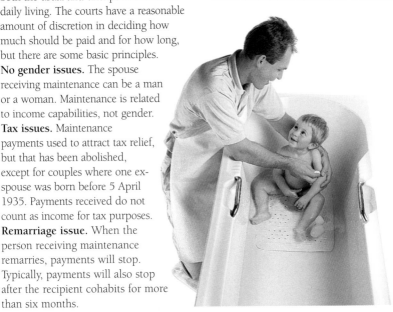

ASSESSING YOUR FINANCES

Income. Ask yourselves if there is sufficient money to enable both of you to enjoy the kind of lifestyle you once had, or if you are both going to have to cut back.

Asset split. Spousal maintenance used to be based on "reasonable requirements", but that has started to change in favour of what is "fair". However, if there are substantial assets, the maintenance could be paid as a lump sum. The most important factor is the recipient's age.

Independent income sources. Whatever income you have will have to be disclosed as part of the divorce procedure. If you have independent income, for example, rental income from solely owned property that you bought before the marriage, it will still form part of the overall assessment. However, it does not mean that the property would have to be sold – it may free other assets for division.

CHANGING THE RULES

The divorce of a wealthy farming couple in 2000 signalled a new approach to settlements. Judges usually allocated assets on grounds of the "reasonable requirements" of the ex-wife. In this case, the judge said fairness should be the starting point.

ALLOWING FOR OTHER FACTORS

Length of marriage. In general, the longer the marriage, the stronger the claim for maintenance. However, marriage over a certain length of time does not ensure that payments will be made to a spouse.

Age. Generally, the younger you are, the more likely it is that you will be able to work and increase your income over time. The older you are, the more difficult it may be to earn an income. A judge might make these assumptions when determining need and ability to pay.

Health. If one of you is ill or unable to work, that could affect the amount or length of maintenance.

Education and job skills. A spouse's ability to become employed may affect the amount or length of maintenance.

Parental time. A judge may decide that spousal maintenance should be increased if child care responsibilities impose limits on job opportunities.

Job sacrifices during marriage. Maintenance might increase in time or amount if one spouse sacrificed job opportunities so that the other could take the work he or she wanted.

Fault. In very rare and extreme cases, the reason for the divorce could affect the amount of maintenance.

Past standard of living. The standard of living you enjoyed when you were married will probably have some impact on the maintenance you receive, but the maintenance may last for only a number of years.

REVIEWING RIGHTS OF UNMARRIED COUPLES

Just because you are not married does not mean that the break-up of your relationship will be any less painful. However, you will have far fewer rights and less in the way of guidelines to help you through the process.

DISPELLING COMMON MYTHS

Many people think that there is such a thing as a "common-law wife" or "common-law husband". Unfortunately, although the terminology exists, the legal reality does not, with the exception of Scotland, where cohabiting couples do acquire some rights. It does not matter how long you have lived together, or whether you have children, the only way to obtain the rights of a married couple is to get married.

GETTING MAINTENANCE

One thing that is not affected by the fact that you were not married in the first place is child maintenance. The parent with care of the children can still make a claim for child maintenance and the couple does not have to have lived together for there to be a maintenance assessment. You will not be able to make a claim for maintenance for your own needs, however, no matter how old you are or how long you were together.

DEALING WITH YOUR ASSETS

It is possible that you will feel very vulnerable when you start thinking about how your assets will be divided. If you can sort everything out amicably, so much the better. If you cannot, you should get legal advice about what your next steps should be.

◀ **KNOWING YOUR RIGHTS**
You may feel you do not have many rights when your relationship breaks down, so get an expert view.

CLAIMING YOUR SHARE OF THE HOME

You do not have an automatic claim on the property if it is in your partner's name – you have to be able to prove that you had a financial input and that you made an ongoing contribution to its costs. If you have documentary evidence, such as a formal agreement or a letter, it will help. If you do not, try to find bank statements that will show regular deductions for housing-related expenses.

If you helped buy the property. If you paid money towards the purchase price at the time the property was bought, you should get your contribution back when it is sold. The sum you get back should reflect any rise in the value of the property, rather than your original contribution. Take legal advice if your partner is unwilling to co-operate.

If you paid towards the running costs. You have to show that you believed you would be entitled to a share in the property in exchange for paying part of the mortgage, or picking up some of the bills. Likewise, if you paid towards improvements made to the property, try to track down cheque stubs, bank statements, or receipts.

30 Other assets may be divided according to which person paid for them originally.

31 Unmarried couples should draw up a legal agreement, which lays out what will happen if they part.

DIVIDING JOINTLY OWNED PROPERTY

Deciding who gets what with a home that is jointly owned is much simpler for unmarried couples. Property can be owned in one of two ways, as "joint tenants" or "tenants in common". With joint tenancy, the ownership is split 50:50. With tenants in common, a specified percentage of its value belongs to each partner. If you have a joint mortgage, you will have to take one person's name off the agreement, or redeem the loan and start again if you are moving elsewhere.

ANTICIPATING OTHER COSTS

There are other costs associated with divorce that should be taken into account, such as court documentation and the effects of taxes. You will also need to plan for your financial future.

SPLITTING ASSETS AND TAX

The married couple's allowance was abolished on 5 April 2000, except for marriages where at least one spouse was born before 6 April 1935. Property and assets can be transferred between spouses with no tax liabilities. However, divorce changes the situation. Your solicitor and accountant will advise you, but you should be aware of the implications if you are trying to get divorced without professional help.

DECIDING WHEN YOU SEPARATED

For income and capital gains tax (CGT) purposes, you are treated as having been married for the whole of the tax year during which you separated, even though you may not have been living together at the time. Transfers of assets between spouses are free of CGT so, assuming that your divorce involves assets moving between husband and wife, there could be unwelcome CGT consequences if these transactions are not made at the right time. Also, while gifts between spouses are free of CGT, if the divorce goes through and one party decides at a later date to increase his or her settlement, this could also generate a CGT liability for the other party.

CALCULATING TAX LIABILITIES

If your financial settlement is taking a long time to work out after you have separated, you may want to make some transfers during each tax year to make use of your CGT allowance.

Selling assets. If you decide to sell assets as a result of divorce, remember that you could generate a CGT bill. If you have substantial investments, you should consult a tax specialist. However, you will not automatically trigger a CGT bill if you keep within your annual allowance (check the current annual allowance with your accountant or tax office). There are other reliefs as well. Until 1998, you were entitled to indexation relief (which takes inflation into account), but in 1998 the system changed and "taper relief" was introduced. It reduces CGT liability according to how long the asset has been held. A simple way of calculating your potential CGT liability is to work out what your property is worth and subtract its cost. You can then add in indexation (to 1998) and taper relief beyond that. Ask your tax adviser for details.

ASSESSING STAMP DUTY

When considering what to do with property that was solely or jointly owned, it is worth noting that stamp duty, which is charged at up to 4% of the purchase price, is not due on property transfers that form part of a divorce settlement.

THINGS TO KNOW

- **Treatment of the family home.** The family home is exempt from CGT for three years after it has been the main residence. If it was in one spouse's name, he or she can still use this concession when it has been transferred to the other party, as long as the spouse who originally owned it is not claiming main residency status for another property.

- **Inheritance tax.** Do not forget the inheritance tax (IHT) implications of divorce. Transfers between divorcing spouses are exempt from inheritance tax if they are made before the decree absolute. If you have a will, your solicitor may advise you to draw up a new one. After your divorce, there will be inheritance tax to pay on estates worth more than a certain amount. You can check the current IHT threshold with your tax adviser. Once your decree is absolute, you cannot rely on tax exemptions when transferring money between you and your ex-spouse, so remember that careful tax planning can minimize your potential tax liability.

PAYING FOR THE DIVORCE

Splitting assets invariably means that both sides feel less well off, but the costs of the divorce process itself should not be overlooked. They can mount up to many thousands of pounds, but there are steps you can take to keep the costs down.

KEEPING COSTS UNDER CONTROL

The best way to keep costs down is to spend as much of your own time doing the preparation and to use as little of your solicitor's or accountant's more expensive time on administration as possible. That usually means:

- Getting hold of documentation before you go to the meeting and drawing up a list of things you want to know.
- Taking a friend or relative to important meetings. You will not be able to remember everything, and it can be helpful to have someone who is less involved present.
- Filing all the information and letters you are given by your solicitor.
- Not making unnecessary calls – they are not free of charge. You will still be charged for your solicitor's time, normally in six-minute blocks.
- Looking for information on the internet. It may not all apply to you, but it could give you an idea of what the process involves.

APPLYING FOR HELP WITH LEGAL FEES

If you cannot afford a solicitor, you can get help through the Legal Funding scheme. However, there are strict limits on the amount of help you may be able to receive and the level of income you are allowed to earn. Anyone who has a gross monthly income under a certain amount would be eligible to receive help. You would need to calculate your disposable income (the sum remaining after you have paid for dependants). If your disposable monthly income and disposable capital add up to an amount that is less than the current threshold, you may qualify for legal help. There is a limit on how much of the solicitor's time you may claim, so check first.

32 Your solicitor will set out his or her costs in a "terms of engagement" letter. Read it carefully.

GETTING LEGAL REPRESENTATION

Your solicitor should be able to tell you whether you will qualify for Legal Representation, which is available for people wanting to make an application to court. If your gross monthly income is less than a certain amount, your solicitor can calculate your disposable income. If that is less than a specified sum a month, you may qualify for some help towards Legal Representation. Depending on the level of your disposable income, you will either pay nothing at all or you will be asked to make contributions on a sliding scale. The figures change regularly, so check the current limits to see if you qualify.

33 If you receive Job Seeker's Allowance or Income Support, you do not have to pay court costs.

CALCULATING OTHER COURT COSTS

You will also need to take into account the following costs.

Divorce petition. You will need to pay a fee to file the divorce petition. Check the current cost with the court.

Marriage certificate. You can obtain a certified copy of your marriage certificate for a small fee by post or in person from the Family Records Centre, 1 Myddelton Street, Islington, London EC1R 7UW. Certificates will be posted on the fourth working day (excluding bank holidays and weekends). Alternatively, you can pay extra for a priority copy that can be picked up the next working day (the centre is closed on Sundays and bank holidays). Check current fees with the Family Records Centre.

Affidavit. Taking the acknowledgment of service form, which confirms you have received the divorce petition, to a solicitor to swear it is correct will incur a small fee. Use a solicitor who is not already acting for you.

Decree absolute. The application form for a decree absolute is available from the court free of charge, but you must return it to the court with a fee. Check the current fee by contacting the court.

FACING YOUR FINANCIAL FUTURE

You may feel that, once you have finalized the divorce arrangements and everything has been settled, you can really begin to move on. However, it is rarely that simple, either emotionally or financially. Many people, particularly women, go on to discover that their finances are damaged long after the most painful memories of the divorce have started to fade.

GETTING FINANCIALLY LITERATE

There are bound to be things you would have done differently while you were married or during the divorce, if only you had known then what you know now. Hindsight can be valuable, of course, but it is better to start off on a positive footing for the future by taking time to get yourself into some better financial habits. Depending on your circumstances, you could find it very difficult to get back to the financial status you had as a married couple, but there are some short cuts you can take.

DEALING WITH DEBTS

You may have inherited debts, or you could have ended up having to take out a loan while you were waiting for your financial settlement. Keep a close eye on any borrowings you have. Look at whether you can get a better deal elsewhere. However, if you do not have much of a credit history, you may find it difficult to get other lenders to take you on, so your ability to shop around could be limited.

34 Do not cut out treats altogether, but set a strict limit on how much you will spend – and pay in cash.

BUILDING YOUR OWN INVESTMENTS

Some people coming out of a divorce find themselves with a sizeable sum of money to invest. It may be the result of a settlement or a property sale. Either way, how you invest the money will be important, so it is worth taking your time. Do not feel pressured into making any snap decisions. If necessary, put it into a savings account for a few months while you work out what to do, taking advice if necessary. Interest rates on savings accounts vary, so shop around.

GETTING A MORTGAGE

Taking on a home loan after a relationship has broken down can be difficult. If you have little income in your own right and rely on maintenance payments from your ex-spouse, there are very few mainstream lenders who will consider you. You can probably get a "non-status" mortgage from certain lenders (for people with a poor credit history or who cannot prove they have a reliable, adequate income), but you should seek professional independent advice first because interest rates and other charges can be high.

THINGS TO KNOW

- **Improve your credit rating.** If you have any County Court Judgments (CCJs) or loan defaults against your name, pay them off as soon as you can. Contact the credit reference agencies and make sure your file is updated. Open a bank account and stay in credit. Register your details on the electoral roll and get utility bills transferred into your name if you can.

- **Check your budget.** If you drew up a budget before you got divorced, it will probably need revising. Remember to add in any spending that you have overlooked and take the opportunity to work out where you can make savings.

▼ASKING FOR INFORMATION
An increasing number of women have an equal say in the finances when married, but some do not. If literature or forms are difficult to understand, make a point of asking for an explanation.

COMPARING DIVORCE LAWS

Although there are some similarities, there are many differences between the system for divorce in England and Wales, and the systems in Scotland and Northern Ireland.

DIVORCING IN SCOTLAND

The two main differences between the law in England and Wales and the law in Scotland is that, in Scotland, there is no minimum time that you have to be married, and assets may be split equally between both spouses.

PROVING GROUNDS FOR DIVORCE

The grounds for divorce are the same as for England and Wales, that is to say, irretrievable breakdown of marriage, which means you have to show one of the following:

- Adultery.
- Unreasonable behaviour.
- Desertion for two years or more.
- Separation for two years (with consent).
- Separation for five years (without consent).

35 You may get help from a solicitor under the Legal Advice and Assistance or Legal Aid schemes.

APPLYING FOR DIVORCE

There are two ways of getting divorced, in court – using the Sheriff Court or Court of Sessions – or by affidavit if the divorce is uncontested. The affidavit procedure is much cheaper and simpler, and is sometimes referred to as a "do-it-yourself" divorce. To use this simplified method, you do not need to engage a solicitor. You can get the help you need from the Clerk's Office at your local Sheriff Court, or from a Citizen's Advice Bureau. To qualify, you have to fulfil the following conditions:

● You or your spouse must consider Scotland your permanent home or have lived there for a year before applying for divorce.

● You and your spouse must have lived apart for two years (with consent to divorce in writing) or five years (where consent is not necessary).

● You have no children under 16 years of age.

● There are no financial claims being made by you or your spouse.

● There are no other court proceedings.

TAKING FINANCES INTO CONSIDERATION

Think carefully about your financial position before opting for a simplified divorce. Although you may be able to get maintenance at a later date, you cannot make a claim for a lump sum.

GETTING DIVORCED

If you have children under the age of 16, wish to make a claim for maintenance, or the divorce is contested, you have to use the normal divorce procedure. The person starting divorce proceedings is called the pursuer and the other person is the defender. Your solicitor has to raise the initial writ in court. In seeking an order, you can ask the court to resolve issues such as the care of children and financial provision. An overall capital settlement (clean break) is usually pursued at divorce. The financial details should be resolved before the divorce is finalized, because once it has been settled there is no going back. If you agree on a financial settlement, you draw up a "minute of agreement". If you and your spouse cannot decide how to divide everything, there is a final hearing called a "proof hearing". At this stage, the court will make the decision for you, and it will then notify you that a decree has been granted.

THINGS TO KNOW

● **Revealing hidden assets.** A court can revisit a financial order if it can be shown that there had not been a full disclosure of assets at the time the order was made.

● **Providing for children.** The aim is to deal with the welfare of the children as quickly as possible, and larger courts may have dedicated family sheriffs to aid the process. The financial settlement can be dealt with in tandem, but will be separated if it is becoming protracted.

DIVIDING PROPERTY AND ASSETS IN SCOTLAND

Unlike in England and Wales, where there are no hard and fast rules and courts have wide discretion, in Scotland the law lays down basic principles for the division of property and assets. In simple terms, property that was acquired during the marriage is divided equally – or, in strict terms, equitably – no matter who actually owns it.

UNDERSTANDING WHO GETS WHAT

The rules of equal division are not just limited to property that may have been bought during the marriage, but also to anything purchased for the marriage. Exceptions include inherited property, some business property, and property that the spouse may have destroyed.

DETERMINING A SETTLEMENT

There are various factors that can be taken into account when determining the financial settlement. For example:

- If one party suffered economic disadvantage from marriage or from bringing up the children.
- Children under 16 years of age should be provided for fairly by both parties.
- Any party financially dependent on the other during the marriage may be awarded a cushioning provision (aliment), for up to three years, to enable that person to retrain for employment, if necessary, and adjust.
- Provision can be made to offset the effects of serious financial hardship that will result from the divorce.

◀ **SPLITTING THE HOME**
Some women think that if they did not jointly own their home during the marriage, it may be difficult to make a claim, but that is not the case.

SPLITTING ASSETS

Dividing assets is not as straightforward as it might appear. For example, business property is generally excluded, but under some circumstances it can be classed as matrimonial property. If you are in any doubt, you should seek expert legal advice.

DECIDING WHO OWNS THE HOME

Many solicitors say that clients regularly ask them whether moving out of the home in the run-up to divorce will damage their claim or mean they are giving up their rights. It is not the case. Also, the family home may not necessarily be the matrimonial home. If it was bought during marriage, it will be, but if you or your spouse bought your home several years before you married, it probably would not be classed as such. It does not matter in whose name matrimonial property is owned, it still comes under the equitable splitting rules.

37 Only a small percentage of divorces go to court and mediation is becoming more popular.

PAYING FOR THE CHILDREN

The CSA has largely removed the courts' jurisdiction over child maintenance. Spouses can only deal with maintenance through the CSA or by agreeing it themselves and putting it in the minute of agreement. With a minute of agreement, you can fix the maintenance rate between you, but the onus is on the parent with care of the children to collect and – if necessary – chase it up. If domestic violence is involved, then going through the CSA is a better option because the CSA calculates how much is due and enforces it, but you have less control over the amounts.

36 Scotland has a clean break system, to enable both parties to live without depending financially on the ex-spouse.

SHARING THE PENSION

The value of the pension is taken into account and can be split at the time of divorce. However, it only relates to the pension that was accumulated while you were married. Calculations can be complex, so ask the pension provider (or trustees if it is a company scheme) for a valuation.

DIVORCING IN NORTHERN IRELAND

The divorce system in Northern Ireland has many similarities to the system in England and Wales, but the procedure is not the same. For a start, couples cannot get divorced until they have been married for two years.

PROVING GROUNDS FOR DIVORCE

As with England, Wales, and Scotland, you can only get divorced in Northern Ireland on the grounds that your marriage has broken down irretrievably, due to adultery, unreasonable behaviour, desertion for two years or more, separation for two years (with consent from the spouse), or separation for five years or more (without consent).

STARTING THE DIVORCE PROCESS

In Northern Ireland you can get divorced in the county court or the high court. Most divorces are heard in the county courts, but financial settlements tend to be dealt with in the high court. The summons for the divorce is lodged in court, together with a supporting affidavit. You will then be given a date for the directions hearing. Your spouse will have to file the affidavit within 21 days and then the orders for mutual discovery are made, where both spouses disclose assets at the same time. You can return to the court for a variety of reasons if necessary. For example, you could return to court if one spouse is delaying or not handing over documents.

---

38 Few divorce cases get to the stage of a full hearing. Around 90% of cases settle beforehand.

ATTENDING THE HEARING

Once the court has all the information, a date is fixed for the hearing of the application. This can take anything from two to six months. The petitioner has to give evidence in person, in front of the judge (or master), but hearings are in private and designed to be as informal as possible. A *decree nisi* can be granted after the hearing and, as in England and Wales, the petitioner can apply for a decree absolute after six weeks.

DIVIDING ASSETS

If the family home was owned by one spouse, the other spouse may still have a claim on it. With pensions, courts have to take the value of the pension fund into account when deciding financial settlements. As in England and Wales, several different options exist in Northern Ireland, including offsetting or earmarking pensions, and pensions sharing. Offsetting pensions and pensions sharing is more common with younger couples, while earmarking pensions may be suitable for people near retirement.

SUPPORTING THE CHILDREN

The CSA assesses child maintenance claims in Northern Ireland in a similar way to the procedure in England and Wales. If you are receiving certain benefits (including Income Support and Job Seeker's Allowance), you have to use the CSA for maintenance assessments.

CLAIMING SPOUSAL MAINTENANCE

Generally, many solicitors advise getting a nominal maintenance, which can be as little as a few pence a month, because it keeps open the right to top up the agreement in the future. However, most maintenance payments tend to be paid in a lump sum rather than in instalments, especially with younger couples.

INDEX

ACKNOWLEDGMENTS

AUTHORS' ACKNOWLEDGMENTS

Sarah Pennells is very grateful to Claire Meltzer of London divorce and family law solicitors Levison Meltzer Piggott for checking the detail of this book. Thanks also to John Whiting of accountants PricewaterhouseCoopers and to forensic accountants Gareth Woodward at Tenon and Toni Pincott from Grant Thornton. She would also like to thank Caroline Marklew of Portal Publishing and, most importantly, Lorraine Turner, for her invaluable expertise and guidance. Thanks also to the team at Dorling Kindersley, in particular Adèle Hayward, Sarah Cowley, Richard Gilbert, and Marianne Markham. Lastly, Sarah would like to mention her mother and father, who have supported her all the way, and her good friend Alison Mitchell for all her encouragement.

Marc Robinson wishes to thank Stephanie Blum, who was remarkably giving of her time, knowledge, and enthusiasm, and Stuart Allen for his outstanding skill, energy, and thoughtfulness. Stephanie also thanks Dwight Harris, Bob Nachshin, and Scott Weston. Marc also wishes to thank Zachary, Bert, and Phoebe Robinson for all their patience and support.

PUBLISHER'S ACKNOWLEDGMENTS

Dorling Kindersley would like to thank everyone who generously lent props for the photo shoots, and the following for their help and participation:

Editorial Stephanie Rubenstein; **Design and Layout** Jill Dupont; **Consultants** Nick Clemente; Skeeter; **Indexer** Caroline Curtis; **Proofreader** Fiona Biggs; **Photography** Anthony Nex; **Photographers' assistant** Damon Dulas; **Models** Stephanie Rose; Anthony Nex; Kristine Nex; **Picture researcher** Mark Dennis; Sam Ruston; **Special thanks to** Teresa Clavasquin for her generous support and assistance.

AUTHORS' BIOGRAPHIES

Sarah Pennells is a personal finance journalist who writes for a variety of magazines and newspapers and reports on BBC1's *Breakfast* programme and *It's Your Money* for BBC1 and News 24. Sarah regularly writes for the *Financial Mail on Sunday* and *Shares* magazine and is the personal finance editor for *The Lady*. She has also written for the London *Evening Standard* Homes and Property supplement and *Woman and Home* magazine.

Marc Robinson is a Founding Director of LEAP (Latino Education Achievement Project). He is also co-founder of Internet-based moneytours.com, a personal finance resource for corporations and other institutions. He wrote the original *The Wall Street Journal Guide to Understanding Money and Markets*, created *The Wall Street Journal Guide to Understanding Personal Finance*, and co-published a personal finance series with Time Life Books. He is also the author of the KISS guide on Personal Finance. In his two decades in the financial services industry, he has provided marketing consulting to many top Wall Street firms. He is admitted to practise law in New York State.

PICTURE CREDITS

Key: *a* above, *b* bottom, *c* centre, *l* left, *r* right, *t* top
Corbis: H. Prinz 4c.